Volleyball –
An Ethnographic Drama

D1518895

FSC
www.fsc.org
MIX
Paper from
responsible sources
FSC® C013604

Full details of all our other publications can be found on http://www.multilingual-matters.com, or by writing to Multilingual Matters, St Nicholas House, 31–34 High Street, Bristol BS1 2AW, UK.

Volleyball – An Ethnographic Drama

Adrian Blackledge and Angela Creese

MULTILINGUAL MATTERS

Bristol • Blue Ridge Summit

DOI https://doi.org/10.21832/BLACKL3702

Library of Congress Cataloging in Publication Data
A catalog record for this book is available from the Library of Congress.
Names: Blackledge, Adrian, author. | Creese, Angela, author.
Title: Volleyball – An Ethnographic Drama / Adrian Blackledge, Angela Creese.
Description: Bristol, UK; Blue Ridge Summit: Multilingual Matters, 2021. | Includes biblio-
   graphical references. | Summary: "In this book research in process and research findings are
   represented in a play script which brings vividly to life both ethnographic research methods
   and communication in the world of sport. This highly original book brings innovation and
   imagination to the representation of language in social life" – Provided by publisher.
Identifiers: LCCN 2021022382 (print) | LCCN 2021022383 (ebook) | ISBN 9781800413696
   (paperback) | ISBN 9781800413702 (hardback) | ISBN 9781800413719 (pdf) | ISBN
   9781800413726 (epub)
Subjects: LCSH: Intercultural communication–Drama. | Multilingual communication–Drama. |
   Volleyball players–Language–Drama.
Classification: LCC P94.6 .B58 2021 (print) | LCC P94.6 (ebook) | DDC 303.48/2–dc23 LC record
   available at https://lccn.loc.gov/2021022382
LC ebook record available at https://lccn.loc.gov/2021022383

British Library Cataloguing in Publication Data
A catalogue entry for this book is available from the British Library.

ISBN-13: 978-1-80041-370-2 (hbk)
ISBN-13: 978-1-80041-369-6 (pbk)

Multilingual Matters
UK: St Nicholas House, 31-34 High Street, Bristol BS1 2AW, UK.
USA: NBN, Blue Ridge Summit, PA, USA.

Website: www.multilingual-matters.com
Twitter: Multi_Ling_Mat
Facebook: https://www.facebook.com/multilingualmatters
Blog: www.channelviewpublications.wordpress.com

The policy of Multilingual Matters/Channel View Publications is to use papers that are natural,
renewable and recyclable products, made from wood grown in sustainable forests. In the manufac-
turing process of our books, and to further support our policy, preference is given to printers that
have FSC and PEFC Chain of Custody certification. The FSC and/or PEFC logos will appear on
those books where full certification has been granted to the printer concerned.

Typeset by R. J. Footring Ltd, Derby, UK.
Printed and bound in the UK by the CPI Books Group Ltd.
Printed and bound in the US by NBN.

Contents

Preface

This script is adapted from ethnographic research material collected as we observed a volleyball team. The observations were part of a four-year Arts and Humanities Research Council-funded project, 'Translation and Translanguaging. Investigating Linguistic and Cultural Transformations in Superdiverse Wards in Four UK Cities' (TLANG). The interdisciplinary research programme developed new understandings of multilingual interaction in cities in the UK. The volleyball team's coach was originally from Hong Kong, with players from France, Germany, Indonesia, Iran, Malaysia, the Philippines, Romania, Rwanda, Spain, Taiwan and the UK. We spent time with the team to enhance our knowledge of how people communicate when they bring into contact different biographies, backgrounds and languages.

We observed volleyball coaching sessions and matches for 16 weeks. We wrote field notes, made audio-recordings and video-recordings, took photographs, collected online and digital material, including from social media, and interviewed the coach and the players. We regularly presented emergent research outcomes to the coach for his comments and feedback. Throughout the field work we met weekly with researcher Rachel Hu to discuss excerpts from the data sets. In these meetings we annotated field notes and transcripts, and analysed video-recordings. This initial analysis informed writing of summaries, vignettes and reports. *Volleyball – An Ethnographic Drama* is made out of selected audio-recordings, video-recordings, field notes, interviews, summaries, vignettes and research reports. It is also made out of imagination. The drama is not naturalistic. In Act I, unable to keep the attention of a government minister, three academic researchers burst into passionate, rhythmic discourse about the game of volleyball. Throughout, the researchers speak directly to the audience, removing the 'fourth wall' which conventionally separates stage and audience. Dance is introduced into the drama, as the volleyball coach and players briefly become characters in a Broadway musical chorus line, or a ballet company. The researchers speak aloud their observational field notes, which in performance are spoken stage directions, pre-empting and presenting the actions of the players. At times, the researchers speak simultaneously with the character of the player or coach they are observing, completing their lines. They also synchronise with the actions of players and coach in simultaneous movement. That is, when speaking synchronously with the player, the researcher also physically shadows the player. Simultaneous action and speech show the researchers showing the action to the audience. The script is of course principally to be performed rather than read. At some points the text may appear to be repetitious, with words, phrases, and sentences apparently repeated by different characters. In fact these are not instances of repetition, but of simultaneous speech, as more than one character speaks the same words at the same time. The start of simultaneous speech is indicated in the text by [//].

This text is not a literal or realistic account of what we saw and heard in the sports hall with the volleyball team. It is an artistic means of making visible the social practice of ordinary life, so that it is revealed to the audience. By creating an artistic representation of social action, ethnographic drama makes the familiar strange, and the strange familiar. It moves beyond the already known, intensifying and clarifying observed experience through performance. It is here that ethnographic drama has rich potential for the future of ethnographic research.

Acknowledgements

This work was supported by the Arts and Humanities Research Council (1 April 2014– March 2018) as a Translating Cultures Large Grant: 'Translation and Trans-languaging. Investigating Linguistic and Cultural Transformations in Superdiverse Wards in Four UK Cities' ((AH/L007096/1) £1,973,527), Principal Investigator, Angela Creese. With Mike Baynham, Adrian Blackledge, Jessica Bradley, John Callaghan, Lisa Goodson, Ian Grosvenor, Amal Hallak, Jolana Hanusova, Rachel Hu, Daria Jankowicz-Pytel, Agnieszka Lyons, Bharat Malkani, Sarah Martin, Emilee Moore De Luca, Li Wei, Jenny Phillimore, Mike Robinson, Frances Rock, James Simpson, Caroline Tagg, Jaspreet Kaur Takhi, Janice Thompson, Kiran Trehan, Piotr Wegorowski and Zhu Hua. Further information about the research project is available here: https://tlang.org.uk.

This book was written while Adrian Blackledge and Angela Creese were Distinguished Visiting Fellows at the Advanced Research Collaborative, The Graduate Center, City University of New York, in 2020. We are very grateful for the opportunity for a period of sustained scholarship at CUNY.

Thanks to Rachel Hu for her invaluable contribution. Rachel was a key member of the research team in collecting, transcribing and analysing ethnographic material.

With grateful thanks to the players and coaches of 'South England Thunder Volleyball Club', at 'South England University'.

Characters

Volleyball Players

Al, 34, coach, from Hong Kong
Ryan, 38, from the UK, and former coach
Dan, 36, from Spain
Finn, 21, from Germany
Hubert, 22, from Taiwan
Justin, 25, from the Philippines
Lukas, 42, from Germany
Nat, 43, from the Philippines
Runi, 23, from Rwanda
Toby, 37, from Germany

Researchers

Amy, 55, Professor, from the UK
Ben, 55, Senior Researcher, from the UK
Wendy, 32, Research Assistant, from China

Department for Digital, Culture, Media and Sport

Sally Letwin MP, CBE, 47, Minister for Sport, Tourism and Heritage, from the UK
Sarah Maugham, 32, Assistant Private Secretary, from the UK

Exercise UK

Ed Powey, 41, from the UK

Settings

Text Conventions

/	Point at which overlapping speech begins
//	Point at which two or more characters begin to speak the same words simultaneously
Italics	Stage directions

Note

When AMY, BEN and WENDY speak alone, they directly address the audience. When they speak synchronously with another character, they physically shadow the character and address the character's addressee. They also adopt the intonation of the character whose speech they share.

Act I

Scene 1

A meeting room in the House of Commons. Sitting at a table are Al, Ryan, Wendy, Ben, Amy, Sally Letwin MP, CBE, Minister for Sport, Tourism and Heritage, her Assistant Private Secretary (APS), Sarah Maugham, and Ed Powey, of Exercise UK. On a smaller table, left, are jugs of tea and coffee, china cups, biscuits on plates. On the meeting table are four full bottles of mineral water, eight drinking glasses, a bowl of boiled sweets.

SALLY   Welcome to you all. Thank you for coming to share your research with us today. Before we begin, shall we do introductions? You probably know me, Sally Letwin MP, CBE, Minister for Sport, Tourism and Heritage. My APS, Sarah Maugham, or my right hand, as I like to call her, ha ha. Ed Powey, from Exercise UK. The research team we know. And?

AL   Hello. I am Al Wu, coach, South England Thunder Volleyball Club.

RYAN   Ryan Fowler, player and former coach.

SALLY   Delighted, delighted. Thank you for coming. Do help yourselves to tea and coffee. Let's see, where would you like to start?

BEN   Minister, thank you for making time to see us this afternoon. We are here to report outcomes of a research project funded by the Arts and Humanities Research Council, in which we investigated how people communicate in cities which are increasingly superdiverse.

SALLY   [*Whispers to Sarah.*]

SARAH   [*Whispers to Sally.*]

BEN   Increasingly, increasingly superdiverse.

SALLY   [*Coughs.*]

BEN   Super, superdiverse, particularly when people with different backgrounds, different languages, different experiences come into contact, / and…

SALLY   Quite so, quite so.

SARAH   The minister was wondering, the minister has read your report, has read the executive summary of your report, and was wondering, what is, well, so super about superdiversity?

AMY   The term was introduced to characterise the diversification of diversity, say in a city like London, where people who live side by side are different not only in terms of ethnicity, but also in terms of education, employment history, nationality, migration route, legal status, linguistic / background.

SALLY   Legal status? / I …

WENDY   And you could say that the term defines not only those multiple differences, but also the ways in which people get along with each other in such contexts.

ED   Sorry, sorry, this is about sport, is it?

WENDY   We spent four months observing in sports clubs in four cities.

SALLY   Legal status?

Sally whispers to Sarah; Sarah writes a note on an iPad.

BEN   We observed a volleyball team, coached by Al. Ryan is one of the longest-established players. Over four months we attended training sessions and league matches.

ED   I still don't see the link between sport and, what was it, super …

WENDY   Superdiversity.

RYAN   I can maybe say something – the thing with volleyball, it's such a multicultural sport, such a big sport, globally, you know, it's one of the top team sports out there. Almost anywhere in the world you can throw six people on a court and they will play together. You don't need much verbal communication, just start to play. The game has its own language, the game is its own language, the game itself, you just play.

AL   I am originally from Hong Kong. I coach players here in the UK from France, Germany, Iran, the Philippines, Romania, Rwanda, Spain, Taiwan – whether you call that multicultural, diverse, or superdiverse, I don't know, but …

RYAN   I grew up on a farm, in what they call basically a low socio-economic status family. I'd never been abroad, never worked for a non-English company. When I got into volleyball I thought this is how it should be, how society should be, how we should live. You meet people and it doesn't matter where you're from, we all just get along, it makes no difference to us.

SALLY   But they do speak English? They must be able to speak English, whether they are students, or immigrants, they have to be able to speak English, or they can't be here, they can't be in the country, they can't.

WENDY   It isn't only about which language someone speaks, or whether they are proficient in English. The players can speak English, but an essential part of their communicative practice is the body. One of the things we analyse, one of the things we have learned, is how the body is integral to communication. The body is an essential resource in the semiotic repertoire of the volleyball player, just as for anyone else.

ED   Semiotic?

SALLY   Repertoire?

AMY   The way people walk, stand and sit, the way they tilt their head, the gaze of their eyes, the shrug of their shoulders, the movement of their hands and fingers, their smile or frown.

BEN   We observed that, analysed that, which meant we could understand better how embodied communication is not separate from speech, but an integrated part of the same set of resources.

WENDY   We synthesised analysis into emergent themes, and these became the skeleton chapters of a full-length written report.

SARAH   The 200-page report you sent to the minister.

BEN   Minister, yes, ha ha, sorry, yes, minister, about the length of that, ha ha.

SALLY   I did look at the executive summary.

ED   Is it possible to have a copy of the …

WENDY   We can send it, of course.

AMY   When the analysis was done, it became clear, it became clear.

BEN   We could really see how, we saw so many examples of …

WENDY   And this goes beyond volleyball, beyond sport, to any, in any area of social life.

AMY   The body is essential to communication.

BEN   Integral to communication.

ED   Yes, I can see that.

SALLY   It is all very well, but what are the key messages, where are the bullet
           points, the sound bites?

           Lights dim.

Scene 2

Lights up. The same. Wendy, Al and Ryan are helping themselves to coffee. Ed stands holding a cup and saucer, in conversation with Ben and Amy. Sally and Sarah are in the same seats as before. Three of the bottles of mineral water are half empty, while the fourth is still unopened. Sarah looks at her mobile phone, speaks to Sally and turns to the room.

SARAH   Shall we, shall we resume? Shall we? [*Wendy, Ben, Amy, Al, Ryan and Ed regain their seats.*] Thank you. Minister.

SALLY   [*Looks at her watch.*] Time presses, I'm afraid, as ever. I am rather hoping that we will come to the main findings of the research quite soon, you know, tax-payers' money, accountability and all that.

AMY   Minister. A key finding of our research is that volleyball not only represents and illuminates embodied communication. It also tells us a great deal about the role of ritual practice in everyday social life.

SALLY   About?

AMY   Mundane, routine, individual and collective ritual practices constitute the foundation of social activity, sustaining minor and major social processes which underpin the general order of social life. Volleyball is no exception. It is also based on everyday ritual practices. By looking at the ritual organisation of volleyball, we can learn much about the essential role of ritual in social life.

SALLY   [*Whispers to Sarah.*]

SARAH   [*Whispers to Sally.*]

BEN   What we found, what we know, when we look at volleyball we see socially organised activity that takes place within a limited time and space, which demands order, and we also see that deviation from that order will cause it to collapse.

SALLY   Order will collapse?

WENDY   The rules are transmitted through repetition and practice, agreed by all, adhered to for the sake of the game.

AMY   We can say that the same is true of social life.

WENDY   Volleyball becomes a microcosm for …

SALLY   [*Whispers to Sarah.*]

SARAH   The minister.

SALLY   I am not sure that I follow.

BEN   Almost everything that happens on the volleyball court is a form of interaction which adheres to set patterns and conveys meanings.

ED   Wait, what?

WENDY   High fives, low fives, punching the air in delight, roaring with disappointment, a hand waved in apology.

BEN   Face hidden in embarrassment, celebratory group hug, motivational team chant, referee's whistle, attack calls, finger signals.

WENDY   All ritual acts which convey meanings on the volleyball court.

AMY   The serve, the pass, the set, the spike, the block.

WENDY   Greetings, farewells, compliments, congratulations, other courtesies.

BEN   As the role of religious practice in society has diminished, secular practices have become ritualised.

AMY   The need to break away from the social grid, to transcend individual rationality, has led to the development of ritualised collective practices characterised by repetition. One such set of practices is volleyball.

SALLY   I don't …

WENDY   We can compare the volleyball court to a sacred space, a sacred space separated from the profane world, a temple set apart for specific practices.

ED   I was with you until 'temple'.

AL   We had a player who would never walk on the side-lines or end-lines, always walked outside them, so if he was serving he would walk all the way round the …

ED   Like, what's his name, Djokavic?

SARAH   Federer.

ED   Are you sure? Not Djokavic?

SARAH   Federer, I think.

SALLY   Nadal.

SARAH   Minister?

SALLY   Nadal.

SARAH   Minister.

AL   A kind of ritual.

RYAN   Like I said, I've always found, in volleyball, that atmosphere that you go and you pick up a couple of games, you know what I mean? One time I was travelling to Australia to play volleyball, and then we are in Germany for a volleyball game, and then we are in Switzerland. We just happened to go past a couple of parks and you just rock up and say 'Can we play?', and the guy says 'Oh yeah. Where are you from? You're welcome to play.' You know, it's just that kind of atmosphere but, like I said, it's hard to distinguish why it happens.

AMY   Volleyball requires the organisation of a specific place and time.

BEN   On a beach, in a park.

AMY   The dirt courts of Kigali.

BEN   The streets of Lima, Peru.

WENDY   We watch the game unfold, point by point.

BEN   It is emotionally involving.

AMY   Transformative.

SARAH   The minister.

ED   Transformative?

BEN   Transcendent. The game changes things, changes people.

WENDY   The emotional charge.

AMY   Contained within set time and space.

BEN   Prescribed actions, themselves defined by rules established over time.

ED   Yes, yes, I see that.

SARAH   I wonder whether...

BEN   In volleyball each rally, each point played is a communicative event.

WENDY   Within each communicative event, three identifiable elements – social practice before the ball is served, social practice during play, social practice after the point has been played.

AMY   That social practice is ritualised as recognisable action – expression of intent, determination, engagement, celebration, disappointment, joy, frustration, despair.

BEN   Each point subject to comment and reflection.

ED   I see that, yes, I see that in, yes, in other sports, tennis, badminton, even basketball, yes.

WENDY   It runs through different sports, but beyond sport.

BEN   Ceremonial, ritual behaviour, sets of actions which follow compulsory patterns, agreed rules.

SALLY   I really …

WENDY   Runs through social life.

SARAH   The minister.

Lights dim.

Scene 3

Lights up. The same room. Sally, Ed, Wendy, Ben, Amy, Al and Ryan remain in their seats as before. Three bottles of mineral water are empty, while the fourth is half empty. A door into the room opens and Sarah enters. She walks briskly to sit beside Sally and shows her mobile phone to the minister. Sarah whispers to Sally, points to her watch and points to the door.

SALLY   All right, I think we may be on the final, ha ha, so to speak, the final lap.

SARAH   I must warn everyone that the minister does have another appointment very shortly.

AMY   Thank you again for your attention. We are almost done. We wanted to show you another example of our analysis of the evidence.

SARAH   We really have run out of time.

BEN   It is very short.

SARAH   I am afraid time is against us.

ED   I would be interested. I would like to hear.

BEN   Another theme running throughout our observations on the volleyball court, throughout our analysis, is that of rhythm.

SALLY   Rhythm?

WENDY   Everywhere there is interaction between a place, a time and an expenditure of energy, there is rhythm.

AMY   Rhythm of the game.

BEN   Rhythm of social life.

AMY   Rhythms which reveal and hide.

BEN   Rhythms of the street.

AMY   Rhythms perceived.

WENDY   To understand the rhythm of social life, we teach ourselves to see, teach ourselves to listen.

BEN   We start with the rhythm of the self – the heart, respiration.

WENDY   Rhythm is the music of the city.

AMY   It requires attentive eyes and ears, a head, a memory, a heart.

WENDY   The rhythm of teaching.

AL   The rhythm of becoming.

BEN   The rhythm of social relations.

RYAN   The rhythm of movement.

AMY   Rhythm of ritual and ceremony.

BEN   Rhythm of commentary and evaluation.

WENDY   Rhythm of the body.

AMY   Rhythm not so much a feature of the action of the volleyball team ...

AL   As the action itself.

BEN   Rhythm is the heartbeat, the practice, the rites and rituals, the social relations, rhythm is ...

AL   The becoming.

AMY   Rhythm is about time, measured out in serves, digs, passes, sets and spikes, in comments and shouts, in banter and laughter, in handclaps and low fives, in gesture and posture.

RYAN   In praise and reward, in crime and punishment.

WENDY   The rhythm of the game.

AL   Is all of life.

BEN   But rhythm is not identical, absolute repetition. There is always something new and unforeseen that introduces itself into the repetitive.

RYAN   There is always some difference.

AL   Not only does repetition not exclude differences, it gives birth to them, creates them.

RYAN   Sooner or later repetition encounters the event that arrives, or arises, in relation to the sequence or series produced repetitively, in other words, difference.

AL	Players repeat the same actions again and again, almost identically, but not quite, not quite. There is always difference.
RYAN	Studying rhythms by recording them, interpreting them, grasping them in their diversity: slow or fast rhythm, syncopated or continuous rhythm, interwoven or distinct rhythm.
ED	Exactly that, recording what you see, hear, smell, taste, even touch, enables you to reflect on rhythms, which no longer vanish whenever they appear. You are able to generate knowledge about the rhythm.
RYAN	The rhythm of social life.
AL	The trajectories and rhythms of the old hands are on a different plane and a different curve from the trajectories and rhythms of the new players. These rhythms intersect and intermesh as the players become a team, moulded by their coach over time.
RYAN	No movement is the same as the last, nor is it identical to the next. The same rhythm, but always different. Like the actor in the theatre, each night the same speech, but each night different. Difference within repetition.
AL	Difference become resource. Difference, like sameness, has its rhythm.
RYAN	The corporeal rhythm of each player and each coach.
AL	The warm-up routine, repeated action, taking turns, leaps and falls, synchrony and disharmony, all are rhythmic.
ED	Different measures and beats coexist with each other, overlap.
SARAH	The minister.
RYAN	Rhythm of learning.
SARAH	The minister.
AL	Rhythms intertwined, complex.
SARAH	The minister. [*Looks at watch; points to watch.*]
RYAN	Rhythm of banter and laughter.
SARAH	[*Louder*] I am afraid the minister.
AL	The clown, the carnival, the dancer, the dance.

Sarah whispers to Sally. They both collect their papers, and leave the room; Ryan, Al, Ed, Amy, Ben and Wendy continue.

RYAN   Heart, breath.

AL   Birth, death.

RYAN   Being.

AL   Becoming.

RYAN   Serve, pass, set, spike, block.

AL   People need the game, we need the game.

RYAN   What we find, what we find is that all of life is the game, the game is all of life.

AL   The playful and the serious.

RYAN   The rational and the irrational.

AL   The social and the convivial.

RYAN   That's what we find, that all of life is the game.

AL   The game is all of life.

RYAN   The game, the game, without the game, without the …

Lights dim.

Act II

Scene 1

Six months earlier. A placard is presented, with the words 'Six months earlier' (if preferred, a projection of the same may be presented).

A sports hall. Players arrive one by one. They are dressed for sport, in different-coloured shirts, shorts, shoes, hats, knee bandages and elbow pads. Ryan marches around the hall, switching on lights, moving gymnastics equipment, closing doors. Toby runs around the perimeter of the hall. He wears heavy spectacles. His gait is determined and thoughtful. Lukas makes repeated attempts to touch his toes, but hardly reaches his knees. Nat smashes volleyballs into the floor and wall. He is lithe and energetic. Dan practises serving balls over the net. He accompanies each serve with an enthusiastic roar. Finn takes shots at the basketball hoop. Hubert sits on the floor fixing tape to each finger of each hand. Justin practises diving. Runi practises spiking. Ryan and Toby set up a volleyball net.

Wendy, Ben and Amy sit on a balance bench beside the volleyball court.

The coach, Al, arrives via the door of the sports hall. He is dressed in a black tracksuit and wears a whistle on a yellow lanyard round his neck. As he makes his way into the hall, he is studying his mobile phone. Ryan gives a raucous, ironic cheer.

RYAN   YEAAAA!! What time do you call this? You decided to join us?

DAN   AAAAAY!!!

AL   I have to work, you know, it's not easy.

RYAN   AAAAAAY!!!

> *The players continue their warm-up activity. Al watches, then blows his whistle and gestures to the players to come towards him. Finn takes an extra shot at the basketball hoop. When they are around him, Al addresses the players.*

AL   All right, can you come in closer, can you come in, please? Come on. All right, you can see that we have visitors this week. They are from the university. They are going to be doing research, watching our Friday and Sunday sessions for the next three or four months. They are going to be doing research on, well, I should let them tell you exactly what they ... [*To Amy*] Would you like to?

AMY	Yes, thanks Al. Hello, my name is Amy. Before we start, would you mind just telling us your name, and where you come from?
AL	Shall we start with Lukas, and go round?
LUKAS	I am Lukas, from Germany.
TOBY	Toby, also German.
FINN	Finn, and believe it or not I am also German.
HUBERT	Hello, I am Hubert. I am not German, hmm hmm. I'm a student from Taiwan.
JUSTIN	Justin, from the Philippines.
RUNI	Runi, from Kigali, in Rwanda.
RYAN	Ryan. From the wilds of north Lancashire.
NAT	Nat, from Manila, in the Philippines.
DAN	Dan. I am from Spain.
TOBY	What are you looking for, exactly?
BEN	We are interested in how people get on with each other, or I suppose sometimes don't get on with.
RUNI	Why did you choose us?
AMY	Your team is quite diverse in terms of the backgrounds of the players, so …
BEN	Also, we already know one of the coaches, so …
FINN	Why volleyball?
AMY	We think volleyball will be interesting because the game relies on movement, and the body, so one thing we will look at is how communication with and through the body integrates with speech and language.
DAN	The body?
FINN	What will you do? Is it interviews?
WENDY	Hi, hi, my name is Wendy. I am the research assistant on the project. We would love to interview each of you, if that's okay, but also we will observe your training sessions, and league matches, and we will write field notes while we are observing.

HUBERT   I'm not so sure about it all.

AMY   Sorry, do you have a question that we can…?

AL   If you have other questions, can they wait until the end of the session, please? We are already late. We need to get started. The researchers will still be around at the end.

Lights dim.

Scene 2

Lights up. The same. The training session is under way. The coach, Al, is on court with players Finn, Dan, Ryan, Justin, Hubert, Lukas, Toby, Nat and Runi. As the scene begins, the three researchers, Wendy, Ben and Amy, are sitting on benches, typing observational field notes at laptop computers. When the action starts, the researchers begin to shadow the players and the coach.

WENDY   Al demonstrates the movement he wants the players to copy. He takes nimble sideways steps on his toes, before jumping vertically, arms raised, fingers extended. He lands softly, feet together.

AL   One, two, jump! One, two, jump!

BEN   Each word corresponds to a step, as if Al were a choreographer rehearsing a Broadway musical.

AMY   Al needs a volunteer to demonstrate the move.

AL   We need wing blockers. Finn, can you show us? Come on, wing blockers, wing blockers.

BEN   Finn is joined by Toby. They perform the blocking drill, leaping together on each side of the net, touching fingers above the net. Two steps to the side and they jump again.

AL   Make sure you jump together. You have to jump together. It's about timing, rhythm and timing.

BEN   Al continues to demonstrate the drill, talking as he does so.

AL   So, it's two wing blockers, two wing blockers. Jump together. Touch fingers over the net. Then queue in the middle. Dan, Toby, can you two pair up? Both of you start in the middle. Okay, everybody else go one side or the other. Let's go.

BEN   The players begin the drill, jump, touch, two steps to the side, jump, touch, two steps the other way.

AMY   One of the younger players, Hubert, stands at the centre of the net. He looks unsure what he has to do. He gives a slight shrug of his shoulders, turning the palms of his hands upwards as he does so.

AL   You all right, Hubert?

WENDY   Al told us he normally speaks to Hubert in Cantonese, but now he addresses him in English. Hubert looks confused.

AMY   It appears that one or two of the players do not immediately understand Al's introductions to training drills. I wonder whether some of them are not as proficient with English as others. But they seem to be able to work things out by watching Al's demonstrations.

WENDY   Al directs the action. The drill relies on all the players knowing when and where they should be.

AL   There, there, come back to the middle. Jump, touch fingers over the net, go to the other side.

DAN   Yes, sir!

AL   Dan and Toby, you have to go that side, then back to this side, so you have to do double the work. Okay, can you try that?

WENDY   One of the players calls out in a stylised, high-pitched voice, which I think mimics Nelson Muntz from *The Simpsons*.

RUNI   [*High-pitched*] Ha-haa!

AMY   Some of the players laugh. Light-hearted banter goes on throughout the training session.

BEN   The players perform the blocking drill at the net, in pairs and then in fours, moving sideways with skipping steps after each jump.

AL   Step, step, jump!

BEN   There is something balletic about the activity, choreographed, heavily elegant, fingers meeting above the net, touching, feet landing in unison on the wooden floor.

AL   And jump, and touch!

BEN   This is full of rhythm and purpose, players concentrating on coordinating their movements.

AL   Keep // that rhythm!

WENDY   That rhythm!

AMY   The players have to time their jumps. It goes wrong often. They are supposed to touch fingers with one another above the net.

AL   Jump // and touch!

AMY   And touch!

WENDY   Lukas finds it difficult to get off the ground. Ryan is opposite Hubert. Their timing goes awry, and they get their jump wrong. Ryan is not happy. He shouts across the net to Hubert.

RYAN   What was that? How was that a block?

BEN   Ryan has a smile on his face. Constant peer evaluation goes on during the practice. There seems to be a fine line here between supportive feedback and mockery.

AMY   Al waves his hands above his head, shouts to the players to stop, then demonstrates the moves again, talking them through the sequence.

AL   You block in the middle first, block in the middle first, // one, two, block.

AMY   One, two, block.

AL   Go back to the middle, one, two, block, back to the // middle that side.

BEN   Middle that side.

AL   Queue // at the back.

WENDY   At the back.

AMY   Al's movement, rhythm and language belong as much to the world of dance as to the volleyball court.

AL   And step, // and step!

AMY   And step!

BEN   Al takes care to show the players each move, rather than relying solely on explanation.

AL   And // there!

BEN   There!

WENDY   I wonder whether all of the players buy into the culture of the team. It might take new players a while to come to terms with the mickey-taking whenever anyone makes a mistake, or misunderstands something.

AL   One, two, // three and …

WENDY   Three and …

AMY	The younger of the two Filipino players asks for some clarification from the coach.
JUSTIN	Is it jump in the middle?
AL	I already said you jump as a pair in the middle, touch fingers with the pair on the opposite side of the net. You need to listen to the instructions!
WENDY	Lukas, the team captain, echoes Al's response.
LUKAS	Listen to the instructions!
AMY	They continue the drill, practising blocking at the net, players jumping in synchrony.
AL	And jump // together!
AMY	Together!
BEN	The delicacy of the movements required causes the men to laugh at themselves and each other.
AL	And step, // and jump!
BEN	And jump!
WENDY	Pairs of players are lined up at the net, jumping and blocking. The middle pair move down to join the pair on the right or the left, then jump and block in a four, touching fingers over the net.
AL	Side, side, side, // jump, touch!
WENDY	Jump, touch!
BEN	The players are working hard to keep in step with each other. But there is a sense that as soon as one mistake is made, everything will collapse like a house of cards. Al singles out some of the new, younger players for praise and encouragement.
AL	Good, Finn, // good, Runi, good!
BEN	Good, Runi, good!
AMY	The players start to miss their step and coordination begins to unravel. Nat finds himself going in the wrong direction, leaving his partner, Dan, heading the opposite way alone, so the blockers can't deliver as a four. The other players in his group stop and look at Dan. Ryan laughs.
RYAN	What's that? Where were you going?

DAN   [*Pointing at Nat*] It was his fault!

AL   Come on, come on!

BEN   Intolerance of errors and hesitations continues.

LUKAS   Do we go to this side?

AMY   Ryan throws back at Lukas his earlier retort.

RYAN   Listen to the instructions, old man!

WENDY   Dan doesn't miss the opportunity to join in with the banter.

DAN   Listen to the instructions!

AMY   As the drill continues, it becomes less certain and less organised. Players miss their cues; rhythm is interrupted. Toby moves right instead of left and finds himself in the wrong position at the net. When he realises this, he retreats, walking backwards, colliding with Dan behind him. Seeing Toby's mistake, Ryan cheers ironically. Dan shouts loudly and deliberately to Toby.

DAN   Listen to the instructions!

WENDY   Toby turns round with a grin on his face. He and Dan engage in a friendly bout of wrestling.

BEN   Al stops the players.

AL   Blocking is about timing. You have to work on // your timing.

BEN   Your timing.

AL   You need to concentrate, keep your rhythm. Blocking is not all about power and strength. All right, let's go again, come on!

AMY   Finn wanders out of position at the net. Justin takes him by the arm and leads him back to his correct place.

WENDY   The activity runs smoothly only if everyone moves into the right position at the right time. The players help each other out, pointing to where they should be, working collaboratively together.

AL   And step // to the side!

WENDY   To the side!

BEN   The collective endeavour requires that rhythm is maintained but coordination seems to be a bit hit and miss.

AL   Keep your rhythm, work on // your timing!

WENDY   Your timing!

AMY   Al speaks quietly to Finn and Hubert, giving them coaching tips about their footwork, showing them what he wants them to do. He is attentive to detail, demonstrating how Finn and Hubert should twist and turn their bodies in the blocking position.

AL   There – there – // there!

AMY   There!

WENDY   Al's coaching is rhythmic – turn, turn, right, left – rotating his hips, taking dancing steps with his feet. This is not so different from the ballet class my daughter attends on Saturday mornings, although I probably won't say that to the players.

BEN   Al wants them to work on body position.

AL   It starts with your // footwork.

BEN   Footwork.

AMY   His speech is rhythmic, matching his movement.

AL   Step, step, // jump, turn!

AMY   Jump, turn!

WENDY   Al embodies the rhythm he is trying to instil in the team. Finn and Runi copy his steps.

AL   That's it! Good! Step, step, // jump, turn!

WENDY   Jump, turn!

BEN   The players are attentive to Al's commands.

AL   Step, step, // jump, turn!

BEN   Jump, turn!

WENDY   The activity continues rhythmically, each leap, touch, land, sideways step, leap again, touch again, land again, producing and produced by rhythm. It is mesmerising.

AL   Step, step, // jump, turn!

WENDY   Jump, turn!

AMY   The drill has a clear functional role as the players practise the blocking technique. At the same time, it is almost like art, a dance which is aesthetic as well as practical.

AL	Good, Runi! Good, Finn! // Good, Hubert!
AMY	Good, Hubert!
AL	Step, step, jump, turn! Step, step, // jump, turn!
BEN	Jump, turn!
AMY	As in the initial rehearsals of a new musical theatre show, the steps are not perfect, demands on the dancers are considerable, rhythm occasionally breaks down.
WENDY	Things start to fall apart. Finn and Runi find themselves in the same position as Hubert and Justin, so that neither pair is able to jump. Finn and Runi grin sheepishly.
BEN	Al halts the activity with a loud, ironic cheer.
AL	Hold on, guys! YAAAYYY!!
BEN	Others join in. One effect of the players' teasing is that they keep each other up to the mark.
AMY	Ryan turns towards Finn and Runi.
RYAN	Come on, are you two playing the same game as us?
WENDY	Ryan does not suffer fools gladly. He is ready with criticism when things start to go wrong. Finn shakes his head.
FINN	I don't know. I don't know what happened.
BEN	Al gestures to them to resume the practice.
AL	Come on, come on, come on, // timing!
BEN	Timing!
AMY	Ryan is not synchronised with Hubert, Justin and Dan. He fails to jump when they jump, and is left behind as the other three players perform the blocking movement together. As he walks away from the net, Ryan gives Hubert and Justin a glare.
RYAN	Are you two gonna learn?
WENDY	Although he is not the coach of this team, Ryan has many years' coaching experience. He is a dominant character in the practice session. Hubert and Justin, new to the club and recently arrived in the UK, make no audible response. Hubert turns his head towards Ryan and smiles.

AMY	When their turn comes round again, Ryan, Dan, Hubert and Justin finally jump together in unison, and touch fingers over the net. Ryan nods approvingly to Hubert and laughs loudly.
RYAN	Ha ha ha ha! Better!!
WENDY	Hubert makes a gesture towards Ryan, attempting a low five to resolve the tension. But Ryan turns away, ignoring Hubert's out-stretched hand. Al comes onto court and stops the players.
AL	All right, now change, // come on, change.
WENDY	Come on, change.
AL	It's the same, but you're going in the // opposite direction.
WENDY	Opposite direction.
AMY	Ryan speaks loudly to Al from across the net. He tells the coach that none of the players are jumping together.
RYAN	They just jump when they feel like it!
WENDY	As Ryan is talking to Al, he again misses his moment to jump with Dan.
DAN	Come on! What are you doing?
BEN	Lukas has collected an injury. He collided with Finn when they jumped together. Lukas winces and rotates his shoulder.
LUKAS	Finn, be careful. Don't do that!
WENDY	Finn gives Lukas a sympathetic pat on the back, offering an apology to his compatriot. Lukas rubs his shoulder, ignoring Finn's gesture of reconciliation. The generally cheerful, convivial atmosphere is not without occasional tension.
AL	Last one now!
AMY	Dan faces Ryan across the net. Again, there is chat from Ryan as he prepares to jump.
RYAN	You have to wait for me, on me, on me, okay!
DAN	I know, I know!
AMY	Ryan and Dan successfully jump together, touching hands over the top of the net. As they land, Ryan reaches under the net and taps Dan on the cheek three times with his open hand. This makes me think about who is allowed to touch who, and in what context. Ryan

is physical with old stager Dan, but he seems less inclined to make intimate contact with the new players.

BEN   Ryan again tells Al to watch the players as they jump. He says they don't know what they are doing. But as far as I can see the player who appears to be least able to jump in time with his team-mates is Ryan.

RYAN   They haven't got a clue! Watch!

BEN   Al counters Ryan, defending the players.

AL   They are doing okay. There's no problem. Watch, watch this, see?

BEN   Al and Ryan watch four of the players jump.

AL   It's only Hubert. It's because he's not used to it. They're all right!

AMY   Ryan continues to argue his point loudly.

RYAN   It's crap. They have no timing.

AL   No, they do, they do.

RYAN   If you have no timing, you can't block! There's no timing!

AL   Watch this.

WENDY   Ryan and Al watch as players jump together at the net.

RYAN   See!

AL   What's wrong with that?

WENDY   Ryan and Al's disagreement seems to be friendly and light-hearted, but I wonder whether there might be friction between the current and former coach.

RYAN   They are doing it now because we've been talking to them. They are doing it because we told them!

AL   No it isn't that, it isn't. They can do it!

AMY   Al and Ryan watch another group of four players jump together. Both coaches seem determined to prove their point.

RYAN   You can't have a gap. There's a gap! You could drive a double-decker bus through there!

BEN   Al is not convinced.

AL   Let's see your group!

AMY   Ryan's group waits for their moment to jump, but Ryan misses his
           cue once again, this time failing to synchronise with Toby, Lukas
           and Nat. Ryan laughs loudly and walks quickly away from the net.

RYAN   Every time! Every fucking time!

WENDY   Ryan throws his right hand dismissively in the direction of the
           players in his group.

LUKAS   You were late!

RYAN   Wait for the outside blocker before you jump!

LUKAS   You were late!

RYAN   Every fucking time! Every fucking time!

           Lights dim.

Scene 3

Lights up. The same. The training session continues. Al is on court with Finn, Dan, Ryan, Justin, Hubert, Lukas, Toby, Nat and Runi. A video-camera stands on a tripod, facing the court.

AL   All right, stop! Stop! Stop! Get a quick drink.

AMY   As he goes to find his water bottle, Dan notices the video-camera. He stoops to peer into the lens. He waves, blows a kiss and speaks into the camera.

DAN   Chocolate cake, a packet of crisps, a nice cold beer!

WENDY Dan begins to giggle uncontrollably.

DAN   He he he he he. A nice beer!

WENDY Dan grabs Nat, hoping to find an accomplice in his laughter. Nat joins in for a moment, then breaks free.

AMY   Al begins to organise the next drill, pointing to the players in turn.

AL   One, two, three, four, five, go to that side. The rest of you, on the other side.

WENDY Dan continues to laugh uncontrollably, distracting the players' attention from the coach's instructions.

AL   Dan, you are on this side. Dan, are you all right?

BEN   Dan points to the video-camera, still giggling, then points to Nat on the other side of the net.

DAN   He makes me laugh!

AL   Finn and Justin, you two swap. You play this side.

BEN   Al still waits for Dan's giggling fit to subside.

AL   Are you ready, Dan?

AMY   Finn and Justin laugh in response to Dan's infectious giggling and are inattentive to the coach.

AL	Dan, how old are you? You're like a little kid. [*Pointing*] Can you defend? Can you defend there? Go there. Go there.
WENDY	The coach wants to get on with business but Dan has interrupted his rhythm.
BEN	More of the players join in with Dan's laughter, instead of listening to Al. The coach shakes his head.
AL	All right, all right, scrap that, scrap that. No one is listening.
AMY	Al replaces the planned activity with a different drill that is already familiar to the players.
AL	We'll do 'king of the court'.
DAN	King of the castle! He he he he he!!
AL	King of the court, so this team only has three players, and you need to try and get them off the court.
BEN	The game relies on the coach throwing in a free ball to the team of three, who are playing against a team of six. Points can only be scored by the team of three.
AMY	If they lose a rally, the team of three are replaced by another team of three from the other side.
WENDY	Al takes the role of referee, waving his arms and pointing.
AL	You can only score on this side. If you score on this side, you always get a free ball. Okay, so the team of three always gets the first attack. If you score, you stay. If they beat you, then you have to go.
DAN	[*Shouts*] YES!
AL	So you need to work out how your team is going to score.
DAN	[*Shouts*] YES!
AMY	Dan, Nat and Finn are playing against the team of six. The game is under way, each side scoring. Dan cheers as his team wins a point.
DAN	RAAAAYY!!
AL	How many points has your team scored?
DAN	Five.
AL	Is it five?
DAN	Five, yes, five!

AL	Five? Really?
DAN	Yes, sir! Throw the ball in here! Ball in here!
AMY	Instead of throwing the ball in to Dan's team, Al lobs it to the opposite court. He has a grin on his face. Dan complains bitterly to the coach.
DAN	It should be free ball here! It's our free ball here!
AL	And you have scored five points?
BEN	Dan is indignant that the rules of the game have been transgressed, turned on their head, the ball given to the opposition.
DAN	Jeez! Referee!
BEN	Al throws another ball to Dan without warning, out of his reach. Taken off guard, Dan stretches, makes a desperate effort to play the ball but fails and ends up on his belly on the court.
WENDY	The players on the other side of the net cheer loudly, and laugh.
AL	Come on, change sides!
AMY	As he crosses to the other side of the net, Dan shakes his head and wags his finger in Al's direction.
DAN	That's no good! The ball came in when you were talking to me!
AL	You need to calm down. You don't need to panic!

Lights dim.

Scene 4

Lights up. The same. The training session continues. Finn, Dan, Ryan, Justin, Hubert, Lukas, Toby, Nat and Runi are in regular positions on court. Al coaches from the side of the court.

WENDY   Al wants the players to practise rotation. I remember this from my playing days. It should be straightforward. When a team gets a side-out the players rotate clockwise, so the next player serves. Left front rotates to middle front, middle front to right front, right front to right back, and so on.

AL   Guys, I need to see you rotate. Come on. You are // not rotating.

WENDY   Not rotating.

AL   We need to be quicker! We have a big match next week. Okay, I want you to be quicker! Runi, stay in the middle, everybody else // rotate.

WENDY   Rotate.

BEN   The players seem confused about what Al is asking them to do. Some of them rotate to the next position, but others stand still. After less than 10 seconds, Al stops the players, waving his hands in the air.

AL   Stop, stop, stop, stop, stop!

WENDY   Al seems surprised that the players do not understand what he wants them to do. He walks them through the sequence.

AL   Come on, you know this. We have done rotation before, when we side-out // we rotate!

WENDY   We rotate!

AL   Any questions about rotation? Come on, let's go! Let's rotate!

AMY   When Al shouts 'rotate!' some players move anticlockwise, others move clockwise. Some move forward, others move backward, some do not move at all. There are collisions between players.

RYAN   OHHHHHH!!

DAN	HAHAHAHA!!!
AL	Wait! Stop, stop, stop, stop!!
AMY	Al does not seem happy with the players' efforts.
AL	No overlaps. You rotate. What do you not understand? You rotate, rotate, // rotate. It's basic!
AMY	Rotate. It's basic!
FINN	So we just rotate?
WENDY	Al's instruction is quiet, but urgent.
AL	I want it quicker, quicker, quicker. You don't need to think, // just move!
WENDY	Just move!
AMY	Some of the players do not appear to understand that what Al wants them to practise is the simple sequence of rotation.
BEN	There is still some confusion, but also a developing sense of rhythm.
AL	Good, better! Come on, come on, // come on!
BEN	Come on!
AMY	The players help each other out, pointing to where they need to move next, pushing team-mates into the correct position, making coordination out of cooperation.
BEN	After several false starts, they understand what the coach wants, and are finally able to complete the rotation sequence without problems.
AL	Better! // Good!
AMY	Good!
AL	The rotation should become part of you, part of your body. You never need to hesitate. You know it. You feel it. It's in your body. Come on. Rotation, rotation, rotation! Don't think about it, // just do it!
WENDY	Just do it!
AL	Good, good! That's it!
WENDY	The players move quickly now, rotating through the positions, their movement like a well rehearsed dance.

AL   That's it, that's it, that's it! No hesitation. Rotation, // rotation, rotation!

WENDY   Rotation, rotation!

AMY   Al claps his hands, pleased with the players' improvement.

Lights dim.

Scene 5

One week later. A placard is presented, with the words 'One week later' (if preferred, a projection of the same may be presented).

Lights up. The same sports hall. It is match day. Finn, Justin, Hubert, Lukas, Toby, Nat and Runi are on court, in the team uniform. They are in a circle, running on the spot. Al and Ryan are at the side of the court. Ryan is also in the team uniform. Ben, Wendy and Amy sit on a PE bench at the other side of the court from Al. They have laptop computers. As the scene begins, they are typing field notes. Once the action starts, they move.

BEN   The team must win one of their last two matches to stay in the first division, so tonight is a big game. Toby is leading the warm-up.

TOBY   Come on, come on!

WENDY   The start of the match is 10 minutes away. Al is discussing paperwork with Ryan.

TOBY   On your backs!

BEN   The players fall onto their backs and perform sit-ups. Lukas groans. Toby pushes them on.

TOBY   Last one. Press-ups!

BEN   They roll over and perform press-ups. As the warm-up ends, Al beckons the team to come closer to him. They surround him, flexing limbs, adjusting knee pads, checking tape on fingers, stretching hamstrings, rotating hips.

AMY   Al tells the players to get their game heads on.

AL   A big match tonight, so let's // be ready!

WENDY   Be ready!

AMY   Al tells the players the positions they will start the match. He has this written on a yellow Post-it note.

AL   Finn at one, Hubert two, Ryan three, Runi four, Lukas five, Nat six.

WENDY   Toby stands next to Al, peering over the shoulder of the coach at the team list on the Post-it.

TOBY   Sorry, I didn't, I didn't …

AMY   Toby has not been selected in the starting line-up. He looks disappointed, but says nothing. He quickly collects his training jacket from his bag and returns to the group.

WENDY   The pre-match team talk. The players attend to Al passively, seriously, without comment. Ryan pats Hubert on the back.

AL   Recycle the ball. Use two and three to score. Anyone else?

WENDY   Ryan is bullish, no nonsense.

RYAN   Defend your line. Don't be lazy. Be quicker. Sharpen it up. Be ready. // Let's be on it.

WENDY   Let's be on it.

RYAN   Last week, we were shit. Let's be better. Come on, Thunder, come on. // Let's be better!

AMY   Let's be better!

AL   Come on. // Let's go!

BEN   Let's go!

WENDY   Each of the players places a hand on top of another player's hand, so that they are all connected at the centre, like the spokes of a wheel.

BEN   As they make contact, the players lean their heads and necks away, and in unison shout their team slogan.

PLAYERS   Three, two, Thunder!

AMY   In truth, the chant is a bit half-hearted.

WENDY   But the players take the court.

BEN   And are ready to play.

AMY   A loud blast on the referee's whistle signals that the game is about to begin.

Lights dim.

Act III

Scene 1

Five days later. A placard is presented, with the words 'Five days later' (if preferred, a projection of the same may be presented).
Lights up. A meeting room at South England University. Amy, Wendy and Ben sit round a table. There is a vacant chair at the table. Wendy takes out a laptop computer from her bag, places it on the table and switches it on.

AMY   I was thinking that we might go through the video before Al arrives, you know, so that we are familiar with …

WENDY   Yes, yes, I have it. I have it here on the laptop. We can look at clips of last week's match.

BEN   That's fine, yes, and shall we have a quick catch-up as well, to check where we are with the …

WENDY   I have broken it down week by week. We have observed four sessions so far, including the match last Friday. The film-maker will come in to do filming the week after next.

BEN   It's a bit crazy, you know. We aren't halfway through the analysis of data in the second phase of the project. We have only just started observing volleyball and we're already planning the next phase of field work.

AMY   It piles up, it's true, but it's good, it's good that we will have it in the can, in the bank. The data are not going anywhere. We can always come back to the report writing.

WENDY   Just keeping on top of the transcription of recordings is a full-time job.

AMY   And interviews. Where are we with the interviews?

WENDY   We have done four and I have scheduled everyone now except Dan and Toby. I'll try to pin down Toby sometime this week. I'm still chasing Dan but he's always busy.

AMY   Just those two?

WENDY   I'll keep trying them.

AMY   Thanks.

BEN   So today we are going to present some of the video material to Al and ask him for his comments.

AMY   Yes. Can we have a look at what …

WENDY   It's here. Yes. It is from last week's match against Spartans.

AMY   Yes.

WENDY   I thought we would show Al video of the first few points of the match and ask him to comment.

BEN   Good.

WENDY   When Al comes, we will look at everything in detail, slow it all down, but …

There is a knock on the door.

BEN   Hello? Come in.

Enter Al.

WENDY   Hello!

AL   I'm sorry, am I early? I took a taxi to the campus. I can come back in 10 minutes if you …

BEN   Not at all, not at all. Please, please, come in, have a seat.

AMY   Thank you for taking the time today, taking time out from work. I know it can't be easy.

AL   That's fine. My deputy manager is looking after the salon this afternoon, so no problem at all.

BEN   Oh yes, you own a beauty, a beauty salon.

AL   I'm just the manager, but yes.

AMY   In town, is it?

AL   Yes, Bread Street, near the …

WENDY   I know, oh yes, I know where you are.

BEN   If you're ready, we thought we would play a couple of clips of what we have been observing, and filming, and ask you to comment, if that's all right.

AL   Of course, yes.

WENDY This is the beginning of last Friday's, last week's match. We'll play the first part of this, if I can cue it up. Okay.

       Wendy plays a video clip. They all watch the computer screen for seven seconds. Sound is amplified and clearly audible. A long and loud blast on the referee's whistle. Coordinated, rhythmic clapping of several pairs of hands; synchronised with each clap, men's voices chant: OY – OY – OY – OY – OY. Wendy pauses the video.

AL   What you have there, I can see already. Shall I say?

WENDY Yes, yes please.

AMY   Please do.

AL   I mean the ball is not even in play, the match hasn't started, as such, but what you've got is, some teams, they have special chanting, clapping. Their supporters join in. They have a deliberate strategy to pump themselves up, make themselves heard by the opposition, to sort of intimidate the other side, whereas our team, I think they are a bit too quiet.

WENDY This next clip, again it's only a few seconds long, this is the first point of the match.

       Wendy restarts the video. The four watch the video clip on the computer screen for nine seconds. After seven seconds, an amplified, coordinated chant of celebration from the Spartans players is clearly audible. Again, Wendy pauses the video.

BEN   Al, do you want…?

AL   Again, you don't even need to see what's going on. You can hear the difference in the two teams. I think, in terms of skills, our team has got better skills than the other team, but the other team, they sort of, for every point they win, they come together and celebrate, but for our team, if you look at them, they are very quiet, because they haven't played together that long, and they don't know each other that well yet.

WENDY Yes.

AL   You know what? The other thing is that Dan's not in this match. He's not there for this match. If he was, he would be the person to get the players together, to make some noise and get them going. But in this particular match we haven't got our hands on it. Every time he's on court, he makes a difference. When Dan plays, the whole team is more up for it, the morale of the team is better. You don't even have to look. If you had your eyes closed and you listened for a minute, you would know that Dan's playing. He makes a noise, shouting, chanting, clapping, cheering the other players on. He takes everyone else with him. He is worth five points before you even get on court.

BEN   Can you say a bit more about that?

AL   What I always say is that he's the glue that holds the team together. I mean, he can be a pain as well at times, but I wouldn't trade. I'd rather keep him as he is. He's good for the team.

AMY   Does he make a difference to the way the match is played?

AL   Yes. Last week, I don't think the other team was particularly strong, but their noise level gave them an extra 20 or 30 per cent.

WENDY   The other thing we noticed, we looked closely at the players, we looked at what they did with their bodies, their gestures, what they did with their hands, you know, after the point was over, how they …

AL   In volleyball there is this pause, I think, between each rally, after each point, so you have got time for that celebration, or whatever it is, commiseration, encouragement, whatever.

BEN   So we saw, for example, after that, after that first point, when Finn made a mistake and put his attacking shot out of court, he went to all the other players and touched their hand.

WENDY   Low five.

BEN   Low fives each of the others like a kind of apology, or at least saying that he didn't mean to let the team down. He would try to do better next time. Let's not be discouraged. Keep the team together. Something like that.

AL   It's typical of volleyball, and other games probably. It's so common. I wouldn't even have noticed it, but yes.

AMY   What we might call interaction ritual, making things all right again, restoring equilibrium, so that they can start over.

AL   Maybe, yes. I don't know.

BEN   And it wasn't just Finn. I mean, players who were not really involved in that particular point also went towards each other and gave some sort of sign of solidarity, symbol of unity, you could say.

AL   It's very common. It's a display of team harmony or, I don't know, group cohesion.

WENDY   We can look at the second point.

AL   You know what, after watching this I definitely know how I would like to improve the training. It's very interesting to view it from an outsider's perspective, because I didn't think about some of these things until you mentioned them.

WENDY   So this is the next point.

          Wendy restarts the video. The four watch the computer screen for six seconds. Again, an amplified, coordinated chant of celebration from Spartans players and supporters is audible. Wendy pauses the video.

BEN   As before, although they lost the point, we can see your players show support for each other.

AMY   There is a kind of common purpose there, yes, a quiet solidarity. There's something admirable.

AL   Admirable if you like, and you say it's quiet, but it's too quiet. We need to make more noise. Our team is too passive.

WENDY   Is that something you talk about to the players?

AL   That's the thing. I don't really talk about it, but maybe after watching this, that's something, especially if I could show them this, they would see what I see, and hopefully that can improve, definitely it can improve. I mean, we only lost that match by three or four points. We were as good as them, player for player, we were as good, but we were too quiet.

AMY   Did you have another rally for us to look …?

WENDY   Yes, yes, yes, but before we move on, I wonder whether we can go back to the last …?

AMY   Of course, yes.

WENDY   I'll rewind the, yes, this, this …

BEN   What is … ? Is there something there you want to … ?

WENDY   I was wondering, I mean, with all the gestures of solidarity and unity and all that, I was wondering whether they can work the other way.

AMY   How do you mean?

WENDY   Like, well, yes, in that example, Justin is Filipino. I mean, he is a player of colour. He approaches a white British player, goes to him for support, low five, but his initiative is rejected. Ryan turns away, walks away, and …

AMY   What, so you are saying?

BEN   I have to say, I was thinking that, I was …. I agree. I mean, if you look at it, it's hard to escape the fact that here is a person of colour offering his hand to a white person and being rejected, that is …

AMY   I really don't …

BEN   All that history of colonialism, or coloniality, you can't get away from.

WENDY   The Philippines, were they …?

BEN   Portugal, was it, or Spain, Spain?

AMY   You can't really …. I mean, you can hardly tar Ryan with the same brush as Magellan.

WENDY   Weren't the Americans there at some point, as well?

BEN   Whatever the specifics of the history, I mean, you can't take, of course I wouldn't take an ahistorical perspective, but here is a person of colour offering his hand to a white person.

AMY   Yes but you can't …

BEN   The history. You only have to scratch the surface and …

AMY   But the Philippines? I don't …

BEN   This is not the Philippines, is it? It's here, it's now, it's last week, it's last Friday, in this city.

AL   Could we go back? I wonder if we could we go back a few seconds on the video, rewind a few seconds.

WENDY   Tell me when to stop.

AL   Yes, yes, stop, stop, yes. Could you play from there, just that little bit, is that all right?

          Wendy plays the video clip. The four watch the computer screen for five seconds. Wendy pauses the video.

AMY   Is there something there, Al, you want to …?

AL   I was, well, I was going to say that Nat is also from the Philippines. He is also, if you like, what you might say, a player of colour, but Ryan chooses to approach Nat, in fact deliberately moves a good distance from front court to back court, stretches out his hand to him and ...

AMY   It's a good point. We have to be careful not to, to, to ...

AL   I wonder if there is something else going on here, something about, well, I think Ryan can .... I have known Ryan for a few years. He can be quite tough on the new players, compared to those you might call the old hands. I ...

AMY   You think that might be where the fault line is? That's the line of difference here, instead of ...

WENDY   Rather than it being about ...

BEN   I just think you have to be alert to this. You can't, you know, you can't make excuses.

AMY   Excuses?

BEN   You can't airbrush out.

AMY   Airbrush?

AL   There's the old hands versus newbies, yes, but another dimension of it, another potential point of difference is between students, who might only be with us for a season, and what we call community players, who have been members for some years. They are not students.

AMY   You see a tension between students and community players? Would you like to say more about that?

AL   I don't want to make a big deal of it. I wouldn't say tensions necessarily, but I think there are different levels of commitment, different ...

WENDY   Shall we watch another? Shall we look at another clip?

AL   Yes, yes.

WENDY   It is the same match, the next point in the match.

Wendy plays the video. The four watch the computer screen for eight seconds. Audible cheering from the home team players. Wendy pauses the video.

AL   We finally won a point!

AMY   Ha ha ha!

AL   But you can see that even when we win a point, we are quite subdued. I mean, it's like, oh jolly good, jolly well played. It's all too nice. It lacks a bit of, well, a bit of aggression.

WENDY   You can see here. Did you see that? You can see the first thing Ryan does is celebrate with Runi, who is from Eritrea, no, Rwanda.

BEN   Fair enough, yes, he does, that's true, he does.

WENDY   Then he goes over to Justin and gives him low fives.

AMY   Yes, yes.

WENDY   It tells us something about looking carefully, examining all the material, putting similar but different instances alongside each other, looking across everything before we make.

AMY   Resisting hasty judgements, I should say interpretations, resisting easy interpretations.

WENDY   I think, not flattening, not smoothing out the complexity of …

AMY   Of social life.

AL   Speaking of the complexity of social life, I probably need to get back to the salon. I should get back to work.

BEN   Of course, yes. Sorry, sorry. We have kept you too long.

AL   No, it's great, it's really interesting. I have learned a lot about my own coaching. That level of detail is …

BEN   Thank you, thank you. Do you know where you're going?

AMY   Thank you. It's been very useful.

WENDY   I'll see you out.

Lights dim.

Act IV

Scene 1

Two days later. A placard is presented, with the words 'Two days later' (if preferred, a projection of the same may be presented).

Lights up. The sports hall; evening. Wendy sits alone. The volleyball net is erected. Wendy types at her laptop computer as she waits for the others to arrive.

WENDY The opportunity to observe Al as a volleyball coach has reminded me of childhood memories of playing volleyball. Volleyball was one of the biggest sports in China when I was young. The Chinese women's team – those women were worshipped as national heroines. They were treated as symbols of Chinese patriotism, ideal athletes who trained and played so hard for the pride of the nation. We knew the names of all the players. The streets were always deserted if there was a match on TV. We would talk for weeks about the team's heroic performance. Volleyball became such a craze for us that kids from every neighbourhood would get together before or after school to play. Any available communal space would do as a court. A piece of elastic stretched between trees as the net. Games would start between groups of children, without anyone really knowing or caring about the rules. Then when I went to university, it was volleyball that kept me sane in the face of the homesickness I felt living away from my parents.

Enter Nat.

NAT Hi, are you the first here?

WENDY Hello. How are you?

NAT What's this? Ha ha. They make you work already? There's no one here yet!

WENDY I was just writing about my memories of playing volleyball when I was younger.

NAT You play? You should play with us. You should join in!

WENDY	I don't know, no, no, I don't know about that, ha ha. I was never very good, but yes, I did love it.
NAT	Why don't you play? You should never give up! I am older than you. As long as my knees let me play, I will keep going.
WENDY	How long have you been playing?
NAT	Me? I don't know, probably since I could walk. Where I come from, everyone played.
WENDY	Me too.
NAT	When I was very young, I heard you could go to college, university, to play volleyball. Such a dream, such a dream. So I worked for that, trained hard, practised hard, got a scholarship. All the time that little kid in the village playing for the love of it.
WENDY	That's such a great story.
NAT	Can you keep a secret?
WENDY	I don't know, I don't…
NAT	Cross your heart.
WENDY	I don't…
NAT	Come on, cross your heart.
WENDY	I shouldn't.
NAT	Ha ha ha. I'm joking!
WENDY	Oh.
NAT	Once I played for my country. It's not really a secret, but I don't tell many people, I don't want to show off. I don't want people to think I'm some kind of big star player.
WENDY	That must have been wonderful.
NAT	What a day, what a day it was. My family all came, my cousins, my uncles, everyone. My mother had never been to the city before. We're from a small village out in the countryside. My brother, my sisters were all there. After the match, we went for dinner. It was like the whole restaurant was only my family. Such a night we had.
WENDY	And you are a British citizen now?
NAT	Ha ha, yes, I'm a British citizen now, a true Brit now. I did the ceremony with the mayor at the town hall: the oath, the handshake, the photograph.

WENDY   Yes, I did, I did that too, the test, the ceremony, yes, the oath, the oath.

NAT   I still don't know whether I belong.

WENDY   No, I know, I know what you mean.

Enter Ryan.

RYAN   Ey ey!! Early birds!! You must be keen!

WENDY   I came straight from the office.

NAT   We are talking about memories of volleyball.

RYAN   Don't get me started! Ha ha ha ha ha!

WENDY   Can you…?

RYAN   I grew up in the sticks in north Lancashire. Got into volleyball by just playing in the back garden when I was a teenager. I knew nothing about it when I first started. When I went to university, I tried out for the football team, but nothing happened, so I thought I'd give volleyball a try. I just felt at home chatting with people around volleyball. The cosmopolitan atmosphere felt right for me. It was so nice to meet all these people, and talk to them and discuss volleyball: Korean, Polish, Portuguese, every nationality you could think of coming through the doors of volleyball. It was so nice. I coached people in Italy, Spain, all over the place. Ha ha ha. I kept in touch. We still chat on Facebook. I spent a long weekend in Italy, caught up. So I guess that's it.

WENDY   You got involved in coaching, did you?

RYAN   I got involved with the people in the club. They paid me to coach. Two thousand pounds a year. But then you got the cuts, austerity. Volleyball was never a priority for the council. The money all disappeared. That was the end of it.

WENDY   Is it all right for Al, having you there in the team, a senior coach? Is it ever an issue?

NAT   Ha ha ha! Good question! You ask the right questions!

RYAN   I've learned to be better in that kind of situation. I've learned to make jokes instead of just going 'Come on, you are rubbish, try harder.' It's about timing. If I have something to contribute, I make sure I do it at the right time. It can be tricky, particularly in a match situation, when you see that someone is really doing the wrong thing, and you're losing. I guess after 10 years of being in a position of authority, it's hard to switch. I come along and I play, and you learn. The last couple of years, it's been getting easier. You are never too old to learn new things. You have to adapt to it, you know, and say 'okay', and you work with it.

Enter Hubert, Justin and Runi.

WENDY   Hello, hello.

RYAN   Here they are, the Young Turks! The terrible trio! Ha ha ha! Wandering in like tomorrow will do!

HUBERT   Have we missed anything?

Enter Lukas, Toby and Finn.

WENDY   Justin, Hubert and Runi start to jog round the perimeter of the volleyball court. Lukas, Toby and Finn have arrived. Toby and Finn join the joggers. Nat lies on the floor, stretching. Lukas talks to Ryan. They are looking at Lukas's mobile phone.

Enter Ben, Amy and Dan.

RYAN   RAAAYYYY!!

WENDY   Ryan gives Dan a rousing reception.

RYAN   You thought you might join us, did you? What sort of time do you call this?

DAN   I am in time. I am not late! Nothing has started!

Enter Al.

WENDY   Al is also treated to Ryan's traditional welcome.

RYAN   HA HA HA HA HA!! The last again! What's going on?

AL   A crisis at work, involving a Brazilian wax.

TOBY   A what?

AL   Don't even ask.

AMY   Lukas chats to Al, holding up his mobile phone so that Al can see the screen.

AL   Okay, can we come round, please? Come round, come round, come round. Listen to Lukas, please.

LUKAS   I have sent every one of you a WhatsApp about the social next Saturday. I have only had replies from Toby, Ryan and Nat. Come on.

AL   Guys, listen, this is important.

BEN   Al and Lukas seem unhappy that some of the players have not put themselves forward for the social event.

LUKAS   We have to work as a team. If we don't work as a team off court, we won't work as a team on court, simple as that.

RYAN   What can you do? There's no one here again! It's going to be a cheap round even if everyone does turn up to the social!

LUKAS   It doesn't work if the only committed players are the community members. I can understand that some of you students are here for one year, you want to travel, do this and that. You don't think Friday evening is a very good time to play volleyball. You want to go out with your friends for a beer, which I can understand in a way.

AMY   The players are restless, flexing muscles, eager to play.

LUKAS   But a lot of the time it is an excuse. And when it comes to having a social with the team, no one is interested. You don't take responsibility for anything.

BEN   The younger players look at the floor during the captain's rant.

LUKAS   You don't feel you have a duty to be part of the team, to respect your team-mates by being reliable.

WENDY   Lukas says he will always criticise people who don't commit.

LUKAS   You can't run a team if people don't turn up.

AL   Can you all reply to Lukas by tomorrow, please? It's important. Come to the social if you possibly can. Hopefully we can celebrate staying in the first division for another year.

RYAN   Ha ha! Hopefully!

FINN   I don't have WhatsApp.

AL   You should get into the 21st century!

RUNI   My girlfriend wants to go to London next Saturday.

RYAN   Your girlfriend wants!

LUKAS   You need to put your foot down!

WENDY   Dan says he can't do Saturdays.

DAN   My wife works nights. I have two babies to look after.

RYAN	What are you, a volleyball player or a babysitter?
LUKAS	See whether you can get someone else to look after the kids.
DAN	Who? There's no one.
AL	Aren't your parents around, or your wife's parents?
DAN	They are all in Spain.
AL	Oh all right! We don't need you anyway!
DAN	It's not my fault – I can't do Saturdays!
AMY	Lukas and Al are exasperated. They see the relationships between the players as crucial to the success of the team. But the players don't all see it the same way.
LUKAS	Think about it! Next Saturday! I'll buy everyone a drink if we win on Friday and stay in the first division!

Lights dim.

Scene 2

Lights up. The same. Wendy, Amy and Ben are sitting at the side of the court. Al, Lukas, Toby, Finn, Hubert, Justin, Runi, Ryan, Nat and Dan are on court. They practise serving, hitting balls over the net, upstage. Al watches them.

AL   All right, stop, stop, stop, stop! Come round, come round. I have been talking to the research team, looking at some of their videos. What is clear is that we don't make enough noise on court. We are too quiet. We don't impose ourselves on the opposition.

RYAN   They told you that? All that government funding and that's all they have discovered?

AL   We need to practise making noise on court. It doesn't happen by accident. Look at the opposition in last week's game. They were really coordinated in their clapping, their chanting, their celebrations. They were not better players, they didn't have better quality, but they were more up for the match. They made more noise.

RYAN   You are going to get us to practise making noise? Come on! Please tell me that isn't true.

BEN   Ryan marches away from the group, stands apart, hands on hips, back turned, registering his disagreement with Al.

AL   During last week's match, the team chant was pathetic! I could barely hear you! You have to be loud! It seems like a small thing, but we lost by just three or four points. If we had been more together, we could have won the match, and the pressure would be off next week.

LUKAS   If we don't win the last match, we will go down. It is all or nothing. Either we win, or we play in the second division next year.

AL   Next week, I want us to make more noise. We're too quiet. Every point you win, you should get together and // celebrate.

AMY   Celebrate.

AL   Be louder. We are really, really quiet on the court. We have good players, but we need to // be together.

BEN	Be together.
AL	We need to // gel as a team.
WENDY	Gel as a team.
AL	Dan, where's Dan?
DAN	Here!
AL	You take the lead. You should be making more noise. Let's hear you // when we're playing!
AMY	When we're playing!
DAN	Yes sir!
AMY	Ryan has quietly rejoined the group while Al is speaking.
AL	Okay, okay, let's practise.
BEN	The players gather round Al in a tight group. Each player places a hand on top of the hand of the next player. They move their joined hands in an upward and downward motion in time with the chant.
PLAYERS	3 – 2 – Thunder!
BEN	The players' participation is not convincing. Hubert, Justin and Runi smile in embarrassment at their poor effort. They wander away from the group, shaking their heads, still grinning. Al is not impressed.
AL	That is so crap! Really! You can be the best volleyball players in the world, but if you have no commitment to the team, you are going nowhere. Come on, come on! Let's go again!
WENDY	Al is not satisfied. He wants the players to put more effort into this.
AL	Dan, come on, // come on!
AMY	Come on!
WENDY	Dan waits until all the players' hands are joined on top of each other.
PLAYERS	3 – 2 – Thunder!
WENDY	The players release hands as they shout 'Thunder!' But Al shakes his head.
AL	No, not good enough. Again!
BEN	Ryan is not happy. He walks away from the group again.

RYAN   Are we going to practise volleyball tonight, or piss away all the time with this bollocks?

AL   If you want to play, you have to get this right first. Come on, again!

AMY   The players slowly come back together. I am not sure that they all want to continue to practise this, but Al is the coach.

BEN   Ryan walks around on his own, shaking his head. Finally, he comes back to the group.

AL   Let's go again!

WENDY   Al is determined that the players practise the chant until he is satisfied with it. Dan leads, and this time the players are more united, shouting the team slogan in synchrony.

PLAYERS 3 – 2 – Thunder!

WENDY   The players let go of each other's hands with a flourish. As they break up from the group, Nat, Justin, Finn and Hubert low five, celebrating their improvement.

BEN   Al is happier with their final effort.

AL   Good, good, better! I want to hear that next week, before the match, every timeout, every restart. Let's remember. It makes a difference!

Lights dim.

Scene 3

One week later. A placard is presented, with the words 'One week later' (if preferred, a projection of the same may be presented).

Lights up. The same volleyball court. Lukas, Toby, Finn, Hubert, Justin, Runi, Ryan, Nat and Dan are in the team uniform. Dan, Nat, Runi, Justin, Hubert and Finn are on court, in match positions. On a bench at the side of the court sit Toby, Ryan, Lukas, Wendy, Ben and Amy. The researchers have laptop computers and notebooks. Al stands at the side of the court.

Toby serves the ball out of court. The referee's whistle blows for the end of the fourth set. The players leave the court and go to where Al is standing, downstage.

WENDY   The match is tight. It is exciting to watch, but the players are nervous. They have made mistakes they would not normally make. There is a lot of pressure.

AMY   The players stand around Al, drinking from water bottles, wiping sweat from their faces with their shirts.

BEN   Two sets all. The next set will determine whether the team plays in the first or second division next season. As the players break, I hear comments.

JUSTIN   We are not moving.

HUBERT   We are giving this away.

RUNI   Who is calling the options?

AL   Okay, we lost that set because we made too many mistakes on serve. We lost at least eight points with balls out of court or in the net. Let's reduce that, let's reduce that in // this final set.

BEN   This final set.

AL   I think you are nervous. Everybody is // a bit tense.

AMY   A bit tense.

AL   It's a big match. Try to forget about that. Forget what's at stake. You play better when you are // relaxed.

AMY   Relaxed.

AL	You need to stay calm and do what // you know you can do.
AMY	You know you can do.
AL	We need to play with rhythm. We are not playing with any kind of // rhythm at all.
AMY	Rhythm at all.
AL	You are chasing the ball instead of controlling the game. We need to // take control.
AMY	Take control.
AL	We are not doing anything at the moment. When we are defending, we are not // in the right position.
AMY	In the right position.
AL	Everybody is defending the tip. You don't need to defend the tip. You can // let the tip drop.
AMY	Let the tip drop.
AL	We need to do our own job, play to // our own rhythm.
AMY	Our own rhythm.
AL	Every point you win, can you get together // and celebrate?
WENDY	And celebrate?
AL	You are really, really quiet on court. You are like strangers. Come on! You have to // play as a team!
BEN	Play as a team!
AL	If we are not serving well, we are // not playing well.
BEN	Not playing well.
AL	Serve flat. Serve to position. Watch my signal. Serve where I signal. We need to // start serving well.
BEN	Start serving well.
NAT	Come on guys, let's push it. This is not over. We can // still win!
WENDY	Still win!
LUKAS	We have not lost this. Come on. We have it // all to play for!
BEN	All to play for!

TOBY	I know I messed up a little bit at the end, but it was at the beginning of the set that // we lost it.
AMY	We lost it.
RYAN	Defend your line. If you are one metre inside the line, it kills the point. You have to be there, so // don't be lazy.
BEN	Don't be lazy.
AL	Runi, try to hit the base line, try to // hit down.
WENDY	Hit down.
RYAN	We are really slow transitioning between offence and defence. We have // to sharpen it.
AMY	Sharpen it
RYAN	By the time the setter is touching the ball, you have to // be ready.
BEN	Be ready.
TOBY	Finn, be careful. Make sure you jump up. // Don't jump forward.
AMY	Don't jump forward.
RYAN	Come on, let's tidy it up a bit, yeah? We need you all to try, every rally, // every point!
BEN	Every point!
AL	Nat, help block the middle, // block the middle.
WENDY	Block the middle.
AL	We need to // focus on the passing.
BEN	Focus on the passing.
AL	You are trying to pass too high, // too close.
AMY	Too close.
RYAN	Come on, Thunder, the passing is not // neat enough.
BEN	Neat enough.
AL	Just relax, okay, when you are // setting.
WENDY	Setting.
AL	We have lost too many points because the ball is set outside. Try to // spread your options.

AMY   Spread your options.

WENDY   The players place their hands on top of each other, // 3 – 2 – Thunder!

PLAYERS

AMY

BEN   } 3 – 2 – Thunder!

AL

Lights dim.

Scene 4

Lights up. The same volleyball court. Al has called a timeout. The referee's whistle blows. Lukas, Toby, Finn, Hubert, Justin and Runi leave the court and go to where Al is standing, downstage. Ryan, Dan and Nat join them. Wendy, Ben and Amy sit on a bench at the side of the court.

BEN   The whole season has come down to this. Thirteen–thirteen. Two points to stay up, two points to go down.

WENDY   The players get hold of their water bottles. Al tells the team that they are playing well.

AL   You are starting to gel better. You're fighting for the ball. // Keep playing.

AMY   Keep playing.

AL   Keep it the same, keep pressing. Serve to number 11. // Take him out!

WENDY   Take him out!

AL   Composure, okay, // composure.

WENDY   Composure.

AL   Try to hit number 5. He's their // weakest defender.

BEN   Weakest defender.

AL   Let's focus, okay. // Stay calm.

BEN   Stay calm.

AL   Don't be led by them. Play at our pace, not theirs. Because they are slow, // we are slow.

WENDY   We are slow.

AL   We are not moving quickly enough. We need to be ready to attack, keep the // momentum.

WENDY   Momentum.

AL   You can't just let them determine how we play our game. You are waiting for them to // make mistakes.

WENDY   Make mistakes.

RYAN   We should always be ready guys. No excuse, yeah? We are only given one option, that is to // be ready.

BEN   Be ready.

WENDY   Al speaks quietly, but every one of the players listens. He turns to look each of the players in the eyes as he speaks.

AL   We are almost static. We are not moving. We have to move. Come on. Digging the ball back to the other side just gives them an opportunity. That's not going to work.

AMY   Voices become increasingly loud now.

RYAN   When the spike comes in there's not one of you getting into a defensive position. // That's piss poor!

WENDY   That's piss poor!

JUSTIN   What's going on? We're all // looking at the floor.

WENDY   Looking at the floor.

TOBY   We have to come together! We have to push ourselves! We have to fight for each other. We // need each other!

BEN   Need each other!

NAT   We know // our mistakes.

WENDY   Our mistakes.

LUKAS   Guys, it's up to us, // not up to them!

BEN   Not up to them!

RYAN   Come on, // two more points!

WENDY   Two more points!

JUSTIN   You need to serve flat, okay? Don't let them volley. If they volley, they will // win the point.

BEN   Win the point.

DAN   Let's do it. We have got ourselves back into it twice already. We can // push from here!

AMY   Push from here!

RUNI   No lazy points. No sitting on our hands. Every point, // every point!

WENDY   Every point!

DAN   If we can get one, we can get two. Come on! It's // only two points!

BEN   Only two points!

FINN   You need to set // the ball high.

WENDY   The ball high.

BEN   Watch the spin serve, watch the // spin on the serve!

AMY   Spin on the serve!

The players and researchers come together and place their hands on top of each other's hands.

WENDY   Guys, there's no room for error now, // no more mistakes!

AMY   No more mistakes!

BEN   On our serve, on our serve, serve // away from the body.

WENDY   Away from the body.

AMY   Don't serve directly at them, // they can volley.

BEN   They can volley.

AMY   Come on, let's go!!

The players and researchers move their joined hands in an upward and downward motion in time with the chant.

WENDY

BEN

AMY   } 3 – 2 – Thunder!

PLAYERS

Lights dim.

Scene 5

Lights up. The same. The match has ended. The players leave the court and go to where Al is standing, downstage. They form a tight circle, arms around each other's shoulders. Wendy, Ben and Amy continue to write field notes.

WENDY As a researcher it is not my job to support the team. I'm here to observe and record the interactions of the players and the coach. But it is difficult to remain detached. The players are delighted that they have won. For those who will return home before next season, it may not matter too much that the team is not going to be relegated. But for the long-term players like Lukas, Toby, Ryan, Dan and Nat, it is important. They will continue to play first-division volleyball. As for Al, he will be relieved that the team has survived.

AMY With their arms round each other's shoulders, the players repeatedly jump together in exuberant celebration, their movement coordinated with a loud, rhythmic chant.

PLAYERS Thunder! Thunder! Thunder! Thunder! Thunder! Thunder! Thunder!

BEN Al is about to speak when Ryan interrupts.

RYAN You just got a little tight at the end, gentlemen, yeah?

AL Guys, I just want to say something before you leave. You played well tonight. You stuck together, you played for each other, you came through. The opposition were strong. They passed well. They had good attackers. They played a good game, but we had enough to win the day. I'm proud of you all.

RYAN We left it a bit too close for me. We could have saved ourselves some tension at the end. We could be better. We can always be better.

AMY Al claps his hands to signal the end of the post-mortem. The players release their arms.

TOBY What's happening with the social?

LUKAS How many of you are coming tomorrow night?

BEN No one raises a hand.

RYAN	Come on! What's wrong with you?
LUKAS	Come on!
RYAN	We have to go out and celebrate!
BEN	Justin shrugs. Runi shakes his head.
LUKAS	It's a couple of pints of lager and a chicken tikka masala! What's not to like? Come on, for the team!
TOBY	Lukas has even promised to buy the beer!
LUKAS	All right, okay, if that's how it is, we will have to reschedule. Have a look at your diaries. I will send you a WhatsApp.
BEN	Ryan shakes his head furiously.
RYAN	Fucking ridiculous!
WENDY	The players start to drift away from the sports hall. Soon, only Al, Ryan and Justin remain. Justin is looking for something in his sports bag. Ryan speaks to Al.
RYAN	We lost points on reception today. There were a lot of balls I thought I should take, but actually you can't, because what would you do? Should I step across in front of Justin?
AL	The thing is, Justin passes well.
RYAN	No, I disagree. You have to be there on court, with the middles we've got, you need a better passer.
AL	That's not what I saw, not when Justin was passing. I thought his passing was good. It was good.
WENDY	Justin zips up his bag and is ready to leave.
AL	Good play today, Justin. Your passing was good.
JUSTIN	Thanks.
AL	You defended a lot of balls. Just work on your serve, okay. Your serve needs to be flatter.
JUSTIN	Yes, I train a lot. I am working on it.
AL	Well played.
JUSTIN	All right, see you.
AMY	Justin starts to walk towards the exit, stops and turns round.
JUSTIN	We won! Ha ha ha! We won!

AMY   Justin and Al embrace. Ryan takes three steps towards Justin and holds out his hand towards him. Justin slaps Ryan's hand in a low five. They gaze at each other for a few seconds. Justin turns away and leaves.

BEN   Time for us to go. We'll pack things up. Maybe fish and chips on the way home. It has been a good research session and it's good to see the team get the result they wanted. Wendy is chatting to Al and Ryan, as she removes Al's voice recorder.

AL   Seems like every time you observe a match, we win.

WENDY   Oh, ha, ha, let's hope we are a good luck charm.

AL   Is there any chance I can get a copy of the video-recording of the match? It would be amazing if I could show it to the players.

WENDY   Of course, no problem.

RYAN   I made three or four mistakes in the first eight points. You don't expect it from me. That's why I'm there, you just don't expect it.

AL   We did enough. We weren't perfect, but we did enough. You have to enjoy the successes when you can – they don't come often.

RYAN   Too many early mornings, not enough sleep. Who knows? Or I'm just getting old. By Friday evening I'm shattered. I'm up early all week. Maybe it's too much.

AL   I don't know. You played well. The team played well. Someone wins, someone loses. Tonight it was our turn. That's the game.

They exit, followed by Wendy, Amy and Ben. Lights remain on the empty volleyball court for five seconds. Lights dim.

END